Pigafetta
Is My
Wife

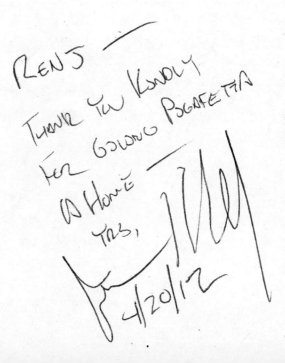

RENJ —
THANK YOU KINDLY
FOR GIVING PIGAFETTA
A HOME —
THS,

4/20/12

Pigafetta Is My Wife
by Joe Hall

Black Ocean
Boston · New York · Chicago

Black Ocean
P.O. Box 52030
Boston, MA 02205
blackocean.org

ISBN 978-0-9844752-0-9

Library of Congress Cataloging-in-Publication Data

Hall, Joe, 1982-
Pigafetta is my wife / Joe Hall.
    p. cm.
ISBN 978-0-9844752-0-9
I. Title.
PS3608.A547265P54 2010
811'.6--dc22

                            2010006252

Printed in Canada

FIRST EDITION

ACKNOWLEDGMENTS

Versions of these poems originally appeared in *Against Agamemnon: War Poetry, Barrelhouse, BlazeVox, Handsome, Hayden's Ferry Review, Phoebe, SpringGun,* and *Versal.* Thanks to the editors.

And many thanks to those who provided input, encouragement, and resources: Lucille, Jennifer Cognard-Black, Jeff Coleman, Sally Keith, Peter Klappert, Eric Pankey, Susan Tichy, Wade Fletcher, Gerald Maa, Mike Scalise, Caren Scott, Danika Stegeman, Janaka Stucky, and Carrie Olivia Adams to name a few but not all. Also and especially, Cheryl.

TABLE OF CONTENTS

Disaster Shrines

Notes

Antonio Pigafetta

Before the Circumnavigation

b. 1491 - Vicenza, Italy.
In the service of Francesco Chieregati, emissary of Pope Leo X—
England, Portugal, Spain.

Departure

August 10, 1519 - Seville, Spain.
Concepción, San Antonio, Santiago, Trinidad, Victoria, commanded
by Ferdinand Magellan. Member of crew exceeding 250. Informal
chronicler, provisional explorer, wounded man, linguist,
ambassador, starving man, conquistador.

Return

September 6, 1522 - Seville, Spain.
Victoria, commanded by Juan Sebastián Elcano. One of eighteen—
survivor.

Cheryl Del Fonso Q.

You.

KNIFE & MIRROR

On the first island no stream or spring, only one tree & only one cloud. They drink
deeply from the leaves & branches

men & animals. We come

to the port, they think we bring rain
we are praised

On the last island, teeth falling out, burying more dead in relentless meridian light

We come to the port, they steal our skiff & other small things

I am Pigafetta, I serve Magellan. I am telling you this story in several tongues
& I am from hell, or, perhaps
some place closer to hell—

here, to be exact

or, silently, our holds full of silver fish, through the Strait of 11,000 Angels

or between us & the hurricane, the fires held
the forms of three saints

Dear Cheryl, listen
when one dies, husband or wife, the other lies on the corpse

foot to foot, hand to hand, mouth to mouth
while the dead one's hair is cut

For what seems like a long time

we are six hundred miles apart. The living
are not without the dead

& the dead are still changing. I think you

climb a chair to hang heavy drapes across a doorless doorway. In reaching
up, I think your head & shoulders tilt backwards

&, by these increments, you are closer

to me, in the pale mirror

scent of camphor

scent of cloves

On the 8th of September, we drop anchor in Seville, shooting
all the artillery, giving thanks

to God in our shirts, barefooted, torches
in hand. Before

even halfway across the world we are
drinking yellow water, eating crumbs full of maggots

smell of mouse urine, eating sawdust, gums growing over our teeth
eating leather from the shrouds

Of course I write a book for cardinals & kings. Of course we die

18 men land in Seville
cargo of cloves paying for the rest. When we throw Christians

into the sea, they sink
face up

& Indians face
down. The cross

rises. Our bodies

sow the world around

A science museum—

thousands of thin metal pins sliding through
a board large enough to lie down on, & you did

to see your body's impression—

what it displaced. Dear Cheryl

things give, sometimes
I steer the car of my bedroom

through the day's wreckage

& you are slender enough to lie between the double yellow
stripe that divides the night in half

Past all points, lost, where cartographer's draw terror

You stand up &, even though it has betrayed you, you look at the steel
outline of yourself

You smell bay leaves & pork ribs from your mother's soup pot

You want to get back in

And where does Magellan's body molder, knee notched by a Moorish lance?
So as not to forget us, those who kept his corpse will trade it for nothing. On

an island past

Palamon: eating veal, capons, peacocks, fish, coconuts, vinegar, a tree's bread

Elsewhere, poison. Elsewhere

the whale bursts through the waves & swallows the circling rook
the rook flies through the corridors of the whale &
into its heart, eats it
& lives there

We cut giant slabs of flesh from the whale

& find the rook at its core, like a pearl in a pumpkin

The rook has teeth, black skin, white feathers. It & its eggs are also good to eat

From a trailer a thousand clutches of petals, my hands

between the truck's refrigeration

& the blunt heat   staggering through

the rooms of September, a man whose
skull has been split with a club

or a cell phone & the texture of your voice

or Dear Cheryl, please
tell me how I entered this moment
where these flowers are from

You gave the disorder of your body a sound
that's the way I know it

What I cannot ease or hold

665 miles between

The 146th globe of buds, the 147th

What stuns

The first pale bud-seams showing
148, 149 hit the sidewalk

What cannot wait
between columns of traffic, 150 chrysanthemums, in a variegated grid

Don't look—

truck & driver pull away

A mouse brings a ducat, less than halfway
across the world. So how is it eaten?

Dead or alive

A bird eats the excrement of other birds, lays
its eggs on the back of the male

A tree makes leaves—they fall, live, walk around

The pagans eat human flesh on the first & last islands
(on the first, I learn why, on the
last I don't care)

The king of China & his women can only be seen
through a window in the breast of an enormous serpent

& in Guam, on the shore we sail away from
40 hutches blaze

while sick crewmen beg to eat the
entrails of the dead

It's 3:53 in the morning, everyone else is sleeping, & I'm
thinking about what you can't eat: bread

cheese, red meat, nothing spicy, certain beans. You are below

80 pounds. Also, what you can't drink: beer, wine, gin
The satellite pivots in its celestial arc. Never mind cigarettes

If we are sick, we should say so. I was, am, bad at this. 3 drinks isn't

cause for alarm   Dear Cheryl, things can get pretty crappy
I mean, with your body, but if

in the Indiana night, you raise your cup
I might be sleeping—& somewhere

a chrysanthemum blossom sails across a bowl of milk

Cheryl, if you raise your cup
I will lay it down on this silver raft, this mirror—

let it drift

I have forgotten our Captain. Crawling across the ocean's surface, hunger
mad—the Patagonian giant dying, clutching the cross

The king raising his cup to the sky then turning toward
me, thrusting his left hand out
as if to strike. In this ceremony & in this sign

we ate meat, gave gifts. It was Good Friday. Showing their king linens

& knives, the artillery & an armored man
The Captain tells the king's slave one armored Spaniard is

worth 100 of his. For 381 sacks of cloves, 200
men, honest & not, die. The winds turn

around us, we think the ships are breaking
apart when

3 holy bodies appear through the rain, driving away
the darkness. The storm passing, to
St. Helen, St. Nicholas

St. Clair, I promise a slave
the best I can give

The outline turning, your profile, in the morning, on the shore, was
a charred length of driftwood. It's unfair

to have to bring your sickness into words. If prayers
are swift, deranged birds

I am letting them loose from the decks of my body
Look for them. Two years

& more promised, seven months
apart, what gifts are there
to give? A ring

to describe your finger or another book
in which to write what is your pleasure or
Dear Joe, Hello? the tools to bind a book

& how much flesh is the book?
& how much bread is the book?

Blood signals the divine

Dear Cheryl, to see you—

On one island, the Captain gave the gift of chains
More often, he preferred the rough equivalent
knives & mirrors

jumping back from their own startled expressions—
artillery shaking the coast

Sign of friendship, scent of rosewater
in the air, the Captain breaking
his sword before the altar

while a black bird flies over the houses, dogs howl & we shoot

many bombards at the house until we see Joan Serrano

in his shirt, wounded, crying not to shoot anymore

Cry evaporating

desert rain before it hits

dust   Green bones

galloping through a sea trench

The cell phone bill
carving each call to a line

Dear Cheryl

All my right hand can do is cancel

Red hats, velvet chairs, silver slippers, needlecase full of needles, Turkish
style suit, six pairs of scissors, six combs, several rosaries, two gilt glasses

In what, as he bled, did Magellan drain the blood of his right arm?

As he bled he touched his tongue & forehead with his own blood
We did the same, &, finally

the Captain gave them a note book, in which to write
The Spanish came with knives & mirrors.

In what, as he bled, did the island-king drain the blood of his right arm?

& who carried the vessel, its ichor, to the other?

Though the cupbearer could have

found himself, duly
in that viscous, red mirror

he didn't dare

You're gone. In the ocean's placid outstretch

the eye starves, hatches

specters beneath waves

And, finally, with tears in their eyes, they gave us
to bring to the King of Spain
from the terrestrial paradise, two beautiful dead birds

Bolon Diuata   Bird of God

born in Paradise, living entirely aloft, falling just once from the sky. Between

the Strait of 11,000 Angels

& the first island of the Pacific, we doubted, invoked that old cliché
No ship would slip over the edge of the world

just a baked coffin. The bawling of infants

of women we took in the New World echoed from the fetid hollows
tugged at that vision

but didn't last long   & in that same hold, swollen

with casks of cloves, the silent feathers of the Bolon Diuta
bob, idiotically, while, starving
or on some lucid plain beyond starving

we round the Cape of Good Hope

Once our voices crushed the intervening soil & saltwater, black oaks
fluted reefs, tulip trees, fields of wheat, schools of fish & corn
into the cement of interstate clovers, they connected

but don't heal, or the wild blade of comment lost
in the widening sky. Hell
is, involved with the dummies of this vertigo

not caring about what you're saying
though it goes   into the silently pivoting
satellite

Dear—

Push a pin into my eyes

—Cheryl: treachery having been discovered, the Treasurer killed
[by dagger blows] & quartered. Gaspar
de Quesada beheaded then

quartered. Juan de Cartaga
left in Patagonia with a priest. In this part

there are long shellfish, incense, ostriches, foxes, coneys
On the top of the mountain they raised a

large cross, a sign, that this
land belonged to the King of Spain. They called

this place Mountain of Christ

—magician unwinding his multicolored handkerchief
while the avalanche descends, bright bandanna

on the factory floor, lambent butterfly

crossing a glacial lake—

It's so stupid & easy
saying I love you

laughing   in, the

nemesia. Can I   call, you

dilate oh   & the beautiful note from the

drones   buffered

anything
you say is
clipped   fine, Dear
Cheryl—

What Magellan wanted, I observed, was two things. One very simple:
to return from where he departed, Seville, Spain

& the second—emerging from the emptiness of our arc across the Pacific
from sun & hunger lapping us up, the pursuit

of the Portuguese, mutiny, & slander waiting with the King—to build
beginning with Christ's blood mixed

into lime mortar then spread across the first cornerstone
Seville—a Seville wherever he landed—& thus prove

he never left that city &, I should say, I wished the same, though
each wish canceled the other, or, I should say

I fell to my knees on the dock &, because it was a dock, I kissed it

Some basic facts:

b. Nov 12, 1983
of Nina & Orlando
middle name Del Fonso
Filipino(?) –

(You're sick, we're apart & there's nothing I can do)

American(?)
5' 1"
up to 80 lbs & gaining

Between two hungers you navigate, bravely

(You're sick, we're apart & there's nothing I can do)

Your hands craft with a pen, scissors, a blow torch, even
welding rebar to brace glass

(You're sick, we're apart & there's nothing I can do)

You have a way of holding your hips, half child, half wily old man

(You're sick, we're apart & there's nothing I can do)

Your hair is your hair. It is black, less oily than mine

(You're sick, we're apart & there's nothing I can do)

Through which your body has been erupting & fingernails tear
your skin is your skin, & I keep rejecting

metaphors involving food, traveling along

the meridians of my mind, looking for something
without compare—

Taprobana

Giailolo

Considering the price of plane tickets: Indianapolis
Chicago, BWI, Dulles &/or National

Islands fall into the sea

Vroza   Pegu

Chelin

The vector we will

Timor   Lantchidol

On Easter, after thousands of baptisms

Magellan raises the host
& they adore it. Magellan raises

the body of our Lord

The artillery is fired
Manifest miracle, the Captain
curing the sick. & the sun, through

the thickening sea water, is still for the eyelids of the sinking Christian

If God gives him life, he will burn
all the idols he finds, even if
they are in the house of the king

The rook takes the first bite
from the whale's working heart

The body of our Lord

The artillery is fired

Islands fall into the sea

Taprobana

Giailolo   Vroza

Considering the price of plane tickets: Indianapolis
Chicago, BWI, Dulles &/or National

Pegu   Chelin

He raises the host

The island needs no name

The Captain arms his men
& burns the village

or the name will be forgotten

The body of our Lord

The artillery is fired

Ternate

Tidore

The motion from which hunger

Which whittles

The vector we will

The body of our Lord

The trade of touch

Motir

Makian

Bacan

EPILOGUES

Here a priest threw out holy water, then the Doge,
drawing a ring off his finger cast it into the waves.
                                                    -Pero Tafur,
                                        Portuguese Traveler & Pilgrim

Mapping

Rage aims itself at any line
even if it divides like from like

& each half already flowers in abundance. Still
a part of me would like to claim a part of space—

anything, even in the coldness
of Pluto's planetary shadow

&, Cheryl, I wonder what reaches toward you
like a parched sailor drinking

the salty image of the moon
& what part of me discerns the ratio of

hello, goodbye, & this has nothing to do with you
in the gesture of spooning honey for tea

Death of Magellan

Fleeing petty Solomons, their swords
descending to divide an infant world

Through the escarpments of the ocean
a path without reproduction

Through cliffs clapping shut in intersecting straits
a puzzle cut from rock

No longer one of what became a skeleton crew
when, through the boiling water, my foot found the shore

I lifted the string latch on the wicket gate
I took the footbridge across the little stream

& snapped a fruit from the pomelo tree

Knock down all the burial markers—
          of course this is heaven

Unfound Passage

That, often, I don't want to hear it
I don't want to hear it, Cheryl—

Meaning I'm bored with the territory of myself
that the county commissioner in my head

has tried to rezone the unfortunate strip malls
of what I've done to kill time & calm down—

to level them, build houses there
That what I thought was a mirror

was a lead window, what I thought
was a voice on the other side

what I listened to so intently
was, on its island of gravel

the buzz of the air conditioning unit
turning on, working harder

Death of Magellan's Chronicler

In his bed, in Malta, aged &, ostensibly, alone
Pigafetta will not leave his island

The world is his wife, his circular travel
the wedding ring. Cheryl

I'm not afraid
I'm sorry I was afraid

You are not in Lafeyette
I am not in DC

This is the moment
where ecstasy departs from motion

Compass

Rage becomes two furnaces
the strait through which a song drives

A song is a line drawing itself
A mirror is a measure of hardness

Flesh is the entered song

The song, the song

Found Pilot

I stood between two trees in the hills of Vicenza
I circled the corridors of our home
The bark of the black oak was etched into the frame of my pillow

The two trees were either edge of the silver mirror
Lord & Master of these figures, I circled the sun that was my anchor
The sun split through the black oak's bark

I stood between two trees in the hills of Vicenza
Two suns rolled in the sockets of my skull
& burned what I should have seen to cinders

I circled the corridors of our home, fatigued—
a cutworm around a rebar
You found me naked & weeping

You said you were eager to discover
the longest, most hellish route back to this place
I said I would pay anything to come with you

Cross Staff

Cheryl, I need to stop imagining that
some straight line connects us, district

to cornfield, & below this line the seafloor
with its grottoes of whale carcasses, opaque plastic

cereal bags & the image of his ship's bottom
in the eye of a drunk sailor

who, during the final watch, slipped
into the purple ocean

& above this line the sky
that minefield

From savaging each other
a thread restrains two hungry armies

This meridian's distance—
it must be completely known to be equally divided

your share of loneliness & mine

Blessing

& in Seville the sailors say goodbye to their women
while Magellan looks to the slow Guadalquivir
Already, I love him

& how you stand on this world
where we erect mazes
whose walls are indigo colored linens

snapping in the wind & sun, an artifice
whose center is this simple pearl
Love, Magellan is skewered in Mindanao

his improvisation over
while the wives of Seville settle for lovers
& the arc of the world remains unlimited

I place my hand under his bearded chin
then bring his lips to mine
This is my rosary

Let us begin

DISASTER SHRINES

Version of Occupation 1: Wrecked Sestina   ...

Stolen, rearranged, amended, made, filtering through the air and light of the
    open door

would you believe Nagasaki was a bowl of doves?

No   My grandfather, a Sicilian
standing in half-blackened suburbs, the sign
stamped between the radiation &

his throat: St. Christopher. What do I do?
I work in DC

on a corner of cement, at my ear
carts buckled with flowers, inconsolable
inconsolable   Cheryl, you're not

here & can't be
for months, the shuttle of my mind can move
as far as it wants, it only rebuilds us in

gaps, pieces   City of
crucified Jesuits staged
from the Philippines, islands where your grandfather thinks through

a typewriter's keys—poems in Tagalog, poems I can't read—
blowing tobacco smoke into a jungle combed
by butchering GIs & Japanese, later Huks

Constabulary, Marcos' forces, scent of ginger
scent of cardamom, Carolina

Jessamine in a plastic lumber sidewalk planter, an orchid breathing in a
bell jar giving fullness to the light
let in by a porthole of a ship of an explorer, a man of reckless movement

Magellan, looking out past
the long docks of Seville—Cheryl

I'm trying to write a love poem
but the thread slips, rainwater fills

the island's fresh wounds, my grandfather
carries a scorched city home, piece by piece, in the cells of his body

before it clots his lungs

Things of the mind lose their definition

Things of the blinded heart harden
to a green point   Through the remnants

our loose bodies begin to gather each other

into a book that is already burning

I'm Really Getting Tired of All This Negativity. Or, Not a Rose.
DC, Winter 2006/7 -

Not a rose but—

(inflected with Tagalog & Ilocano, if I

could fix your face   in

stone   like the Greeks did)   where that
trouble, Black

Mary

& mass in the basilica crypt   (a

gesture, then

)   an uneven stack of books

on prayer   a Russian
aesthetic—Dear Lord. . . Dear Lord . . .
under the thumbtack

Ted Berrigan in classic underwear. No—

kindness   pursing your
lips   No   that you were worried
over a goldfish's soul &

read me Oppen's
wife's stuff?   Wasn't he

a commie?   Anyway   bay leaves
& pig's blood   from the burned ship

a saint, making
lemonade   in rain

that, in rain
mind the best
seeking
a prayer, now

for the Roman dead

You stand over there   in a posture
there is rain   sometimes
there isn't   (oh   play
with gnarly binaries)   you

smash the hoops

of my images   your rain colored shirt
in a pile of dirty laundry

in my closet   & an aquarium we
bought in your kitchen gurgling

but fishless   still

there are 22 years of stone under
your visible skin, working its way
out in—

Your sister says I have to read Rizal

You think quite a lot about G-O-D
whereas I feel the edges are being

eaten away by
light—yes? No
no.

light

Version of Occupation 2: Sestina: John Rabe's Lilacs
Nanking, Winter 1937 - '

—then pierced with bamboo shoots, driven harder
the dead dragged to the Yangtze, the banks piled
with soft cargo. Purple mountain blooms
with mortar: winter, without rain, the river
will not take more. *What did they call lilacs?*
It does not matter. All these things happen

at once. *Was he your son? What happened?*
They burnt his head with gasoline. It's hard
to think they were that bored. John clips lilac—
stacks the old, finger-thin limbs in neat piles
& writes his Führer: *Atrocity blooms.*
Our ally kills for sport. Now the river

will not even swallow stones—the widening river
of night you're swimming while each thing happens
& is forgotten: slowly, surely it blooms
then softens like flesh, your mind a garden hard
against your skull where each day's black fruit piles
During the Rape who thought of foreign lilacs?

Some did. *It must have seemed madness:* lilacs
The mind has room for each thing, a river
even, the Yangtze of your youth—now piled
with friends—so every river happened
on has the dead packed in its mud. It's so hard
to know this as this, that as that which blooms

as itself. She knows his house by the bloom
above the wall & finds his door, lilac
bruises on every limb, her face a hard
knot of pain which will not unscrew, rivers
of blood & mucus—child. *Whose? What happened?*
Knowing the Nazi's amnesty, they pile

into his garden. Stones of mercy pile
on his chest. Gestapo disapprove. The blooms
take places where death, daily happened
They lose the name of his flowering shrub
Gone, he is made a Buddha. The river
unchokes, the dead eddy away. A hard

season piled like leaves & burned, the black smoke
a churning river, then just a rumor
What happened? What happens. Happens harder

Working, with Madness in Friends & Various Flowers
DC, Summer 2006 -

Between the green carts   below
of impatiens   the green roof, with

a tray of heart shaped leaves, & heart shaped petals

with the general fever

on the corner of S & 14th, rain, the fine kind

Who says who is trying to break themselves?

it being summer, & a street curb: cutting
           blossom from rose
lifting the
blossom—from
so that

lifting, in the weakened hand
all is bramble & beginning

cold against the
soft fold of Adrian's foreskin
the blade, & into—

One learns about these things

Adrian pressing the smeared bit into the gallery wall
image refracting through the internet

How is that? Howzat? No, I do not know
how anyone is doing   or thinking
just they are

& had to break the door down only after you told me—

Mutilation ugly so far as we are mutable

so here I am standing in a white room
where the handle should be   a diamond cut into the door

When you told me this   & remembered
I shut the door   when you told me this

Shrines & Incidents
DC, Spring 2006 -

Lying under a cherry tree by the Jefferson memorial drinking
cheap beer out of a thermos, a pink canopy of
blossoms hanging about us describing
how happy you'd be leaving my city, I said
how happy any decision is. At the tidal basin
we passed a duck floating on a street lamp's
pale rim of light *Ducky you're lost, Ducky you are* &
regretted it, immediately, catching

the jelly of his eyes as he turned his head to the dark water rising &
falling. Near New York Ave, along P St. wire wreathing
junk lots, the silvery flash—*Guess what I got*
in my pocket it's big son guess what I got in my pocket—
of a gun. We grappled for hours

in bed, sorting out that fear, watching you wrap
a bandage about your burnt, blistered
thigh, though you told me not to
look. In the face of all this
beauty I wondered if the strong limbs
of a disease were branching through my body, or was I just growing
old. As if to prove this
I received Susan's conspiratorial DVD, sat in my room & watched

two buildings fall down until daylight savings happened (clock rolling from

2 to 3) & it was already too late

It's not that I care about the color & sound of
detonations on the 14th floor or that I think
the government did it, it's that

I want more elaborate explanations for things
& I'll never see Susan
again, it's that we were lying under clouds of
blossoms & I don't want you to exist
in that invisible hour I can't remember when
I first met you, only that
you might be leaving—to want
the blinking stone of your skull
fastened to my chest, to watch
you cut a mango & tell me not to eat it
because your blood has disappeared in its flesh
to say, pulling the bandage from your thigh

This is the first time you'll ever see me

On the Metro Away from DC
Spring 2007 -

What are you doing? *Eating pumpkin seeds & reading a book in Adams Morgan*
or not yet forgiving me or
somewhere stalled in the processes. On

the library's empty 4th floor, below the limbs & airborne roots
the strangling tree, *You*

have your own rhythm & just push
ahead. In North Carolina, I was almost
lost on the

What lives   in silence
What loves   *I know*
loves

That will not speak
the guest, there is no

These things happen: drunk, on hands & knees
on the bathroom tile, unable to towel or see
from elbow & shins, like an animal, bleeding—what

lives in the border silence
in the hacked stump
that could not give

Told to fuck off, playing
a game, pretending to kill
each other—what 2, 3 weeks now

One would have me understand that

if one identifies the correct force
one can invite it to speak
relieving the sickness

urging it to leave the body. Two days
after the crash, on the way to the grocery store—
threat from Danny

in silence, housed
in lung & throat, there are agents who
will not, if we

press the sweat into—*Your own
rhythm & push*— our eyes

ahead—I know   we are
in our chairs   Come with me
in silence   what lives

What are you doing?
what

inching along the border spaces
the city mapped in my mind's blue cloud
Here I am

2 am: pinned beneath my bicycle
on 1st, just below
Florida, helmet gone

somehow, blood so dark
it starts erasing—

& what fills this space
like sand in a balloon. Do you
see what this is? Want

the walls of this room to buckle, fold
arrogant book to burn
& a stranger to erupt in

among scattered folding chairs—

& here we are, invited to speak

with a six pack of tall boys
red candles & the tv shadows
on the inside of an eggshell

Where are you?

the thread through the coin
a can of sardines
& a cigarette for everyone

Rizalian Epilogue

Lightning & the virgin

white lightning &   in
feeling who

foxglove   atlas   long dress

arrives, oh   In soft folds the roofs climb toward the reservoir, the water

tied by the ankles &   lowered in broken   pottery, grey

Silt of his eyes   filmed with   rain opening
around the city, rain

crocus

tongues what wound

will close seeing

the virgin   in an electrical arc

is the virgin
the myth of

what wound

When I woke

my ship was in the foothills of a strange mountain
my crew had turned to ivy
the virgin was burnt black

Version of Occupation 3: A Soldier Born in Nagasaki Returns from China

Summer 1945 -

When the sun opened in our city
when the black rain fell
& my sister pulled the skin from her body
as if it were a robe
her bones stepped out, into our garden
& stood there looking

When the emperor stepped off the train
wearing a derby & necktie, the general
at his side chomping his pipe, both of them
shaking our split hands, as if to say
it's very interesting none of us are dead
& what do we do now?

When the emperor left, I ate lunch
with some kids I knew back in China—
onions & mushrooms
what we could find

When there is nothing left in the day
I cool off at a café, draw a list of people
who are as, & think I should slide
my dick deep into something so I can root
before the wind picks up

When there is nothing left in the night
when I think of Nanjing's heat, flies
rising from the river, mosquitoes

descending from my tent's
steeple, tall grass & three women tied to posts
how my best friend attached his bayonet, how the
commander said "Now"

That night we gambled
& drank liquor we found in a house
as it burned down around us
laughing at a story of refugees
eating every daisy and goldenrod
on Ginling College campus
I lost all my money & so what
when it's all practice, tonight
in a city never my own
I hear the heavy-booted GIs
stumbling from bars
calling for women, when even
the soldiers are satisfied, sleep comes
when even sleep comes, I think of my sister
& know she won't reflower from the ground
where I think they might have stuck her—

So that what I miss most
is the peach tree my parents planted
between the sea & my window
with the city & harbor swallowed
nothing to take, nothing to save
not even a peach pit
not even dirt

So that when I wake in the night
the orphan breaks into my mind
the one I saw at Shinagawa Station
a white sash knotted at her neck
& cinched around a chest high box

which carried her family
their cremated bones
& how jealous I am
she held herself square as a soldier

Primus Circumdedesti Me: Return Trip to DC after Helping You Move to Indiana

Summer, 2007 -

Taxiing again, fight off   & slicing through
the cloud banks   the night train pulling

thick haze, lifting into
hollow, now

of away

White
or shell

water tower's crown, luminous necklace of a warehouse, acres quarantined

horizon, 2 meridians of   washed out blue, bleeding
Margin, the   other bright edge

of this is where I try &
receiver, in/of, think or   a final

bending
phenomena

Blossom fading into three coordinates
the outlying ripple faltering or

Breaking on   in burnt space

where St. Christopher & my grandfather crouch in

perforated shadows, city withered & eaten as corn in

drought, where, between two occupying armies
your grandfather blows smoke through a dark window

feeling a pattern
which, I don't know why

it does, it blisters

. . .

St. Christopher, Our Lady of Providence

the houses' pale faces flare up

St. Scraped Frame
St.—

. . .

The locomotive enters the dim mass

where I'm supposed to think of the end of the body

& the window laying on the bed a honeycomb of light, or is this
where I'm supposed to mention god, the tremor
of a passing freight eating the tracks?

Water spilling from a bent pipe

If the world is a glass tree, is a
The engine probes

the hand in my lap

joints   the assemblage   steel

& combustible fuel
the earth sails

through an ocean trench, the porcelain darkness

turning in the fragrant heart   some body

in response to mine

Borrowed   ...

The bridge & double embark to open

in gulf
between   fashion photographer, man circumcising himself for
others' gratification & the skin

opening & closing on your elbows' insides—distance:

8 inches between my hand & your shoulder, checking an e-mail about
missing doors in an apartment about to be rented
665 miles from here—repair

liminal space! Voice erupting within
or borrowed in
canvas of

the mailbox standing in the night, circling
blocks around—

Can I have it?   Broke enough for a bus ticket
& imagining the upside of cornfields

Is this okay?

No one is getting ripped off on their tips
trembling   as the word

extends, sorry I said it
Don't forget the throat
on hand
as the note—

you stand in my (our?)
or your
doorway &
what was right here is

or, to ceiling & floor
the opening throat, St. Christopher

San Lorenzo Ruiz, cross that flowers
or cross that sweats, the old ghosts

bringing forward their altar in the grove or wherever
the old frame

holds up its dehydrated garlands
the wounds of pierced deities

what takes possession
you, holding

a fork over a plate of squash peels   behind the register
the saffron air from the street window, cars ploughing parallel on R &
diagonally away down

Florida, that shuffle of what was to—everyone says

it's a "dick-shaped" scar forming on the inside
of my elbow from the bike crash

says "whatever that means"—who disfigures
for show or accident, makes way for

or open to whatever monstrous idea embroiders the air
or I'm about to get you

a can of sardines!

Poem with Language of Martyrdom from DeMorga's Account of the Japanese Emperor's Orders RE: Missionaries Sent from the Philippines

. . . Summer -

Their right ears were cut off
they were paraded through the streets   to the great grief

& sorrow of all Christians
who saw their suffering, come   closer, the July

sun, scent of dried leaves from my forearms
come closer   in Nangasaqui
all crucified in a row, with iron
staples at their throats, hands &
feet   come
closer, divide the heat, up 1st
not lonely, but burned   come

closer   Farewell, Doctor!
Farewell!!   Our Lord
not regarding my sins, has   in His mercy
made me one of 24
who are about to die
for love of Him   up the stairs, past

my potted tomatoes, sweet potatoes, Cuban oregano

where your foot falls

It's not that I'm waiting
not that you're lying in bed reading
about one of Marquez's pilgrims

or the endless Jesus prayer
in your floral underwear—

Storax, gum-resin, as perfume, before the shroud
is wrapped around, raising

the box of the dead
onto the roof, lowering the box
of the dead into the ground

so we can continue
to ask our precursors questions

Where are you?
Where are you?

What answer—
Over your eyes & mouth

A small gold wafer

When they came to the island
they thanked God for the natives' beauty

they murdered some of the natives

when they came to the island
I woke up in a dress

my hair was long
& a lightness in my hips

all the drawers in my dresser opened
my ancestors climbed out

when they came to the island

we clothed them because they were naked
they were thieves, so we killed them

when they woke

there was no word for virginity

when I came to the island

It's not that I'm waiting
it's not that you're gone

it's that I am also the man
breaking the seals on the funeral boxes

confiscating the bones
tossing them into the river

& raising a cross
before slashing my way back through the hibiscus

into the interval of your night
what questions are left

& what will you father?

When there was no word for virginity

 (a lightness in the hips)

When I came to the island

(the coffins in the trees)

When I woke up in a dress

 (a lightness in the hips)

Version of Occupation 4/Pantoum 1: Descent & Ascent ...

The sunflower buries its bronze face
in the soil, cracked into black squares
which recall so many burned books
so much ash one thinks they have an afterlife

in the earth, cracked into black squares
studding the stairwell, smeared with
so much ash one thinks they have an afterlife
&, indeed, the burnt tags read: heaven. Meteorites

studding the stairwell, smeared with
paint. Cages nested in cages
&, indeed, the burnt tags read: heaven. Meteorites
wedged in giant bookcases, the dome of night:

paint. Cages nested in cages
the milk-flecked cosmos, serial numbered, wrapped into books
wedged in giant bookcases, the dome of night
the rope at his neck, the blood in the field

the milk-flecked cosmos, serial numbered, wrapped into a book
earth, the field of stars, a hand rising from the paint
the blood—the rope at this neck & in the field
a man lies down with a burning branch

earth, the field of stars, a hand rising from the paint
a serpent unable to rest in his swollen coils
a man lying down with a burning branch
a sunflower: the drum, struck once at its internment

St. Etc.'s Tomb   ...

There is the cross that grows & the cross that sweats, in sickness & prudence
a sacrifice made to every altar: Monday morning, I call
my father, my sister, my brother, on my knee, neck bent, god
of recovery, of traffic lights, climbing god, god of
jasmine blossoms clustered on S & 14th, of the wheel turning

from the curb. In sleep you tear the skin away
from the inner parts of your elbows while I sleep my
clerical sleep inches beside. We bring the man,
they call the doctor who costs the most
into the house. He sits on your bed
& asks about your dreams

The cross of Tunasan   or the cross of Matahong?
Saint Francis   San Juan
The cross that grows, the cross   that sweats, doubled under

ourselves, we lie parallel in bed, & turn—I tried to explain
to a woman with bug-eyed, emerald-framed
sunglasses why one would buy a jasmine plant
when it dies in winter—today we're going to buy vegan pastries
If one prays for another then one is

alone—yesterday, pork sausage
St. Stephen   St. Jerome

Saint X, Saint Etc., bicycling with a pack full of groceries
—oranges, Drain-O, Countrytime

Lemonade Mix—on the thread of cement
between St. Mary's Cemetery & North Capitol, moving

moving . Who

. . .

is the god of your father, the god of my father, of the cigarette
over the patio's cracked brick & baked weeds
of waiting & silence? Who
is the god of this distance? In the crypt
beneath the ochre tiles of the arches, between the Byzantine
angles of gravel-colored stained glass
between the organ & song, call

& response. My father
ignites my thigh via
cell phone, the thigh closest to
you. Monday evening

mass is a mass

for those who come
alone

. . .

. . .

Pantoum 2: Unfinishable, with Circumnavigator
& National Cathedral   . . .

In the basilica crypt, what do you pray for?
On the shore   Pigafetta,   in strange motion of hips,
memory of   beside the Black Virgin   .   Lafayette
              confirmed Stephen   Christopher

        her spotted hands   Pacific fleet,   will protect
In the basilica crypt, what do you pray for?
Your green purse on veined stone—chapstick, notebook, steroids, thoughts
      flowering toward
            of   of Antipolo   moving,

of gesture toward the boar's heart   piercing again & again, it
My grandmother   the medal he   ,   sailing   Nagasaki: St. Christopher
would not   from lung cancer (what'd I care)   Chop down Pigafetta,
      give me breasts
Your green purse on veined stone—   thought   toward

The tourist's digital camera aimed at the saint to your left—take this thought, this
this lance revolving around the boar's heart, in her hand   with the dearest word
                between thumb & forehead
protect my grandfather   give me breasts, my face
      smeared with boar's blood

I don't want this or worry, I want, or, I want—
camera aimed at St. Take This Thought, taste of iron
to be Pigafetta or you, priestess or eaten boar, to be
the space between the father's thumb & my forehead, oil which

or, on the shore, an old woman in Spanish armor
x x x x x x x x x x x x x x x
or I don't want this or worry, I want, or, where
you are, I am, changing

NOTES

5 – Portions of "Knife & Mirror" have been taken from Antonio Pigafetta's account of Magellan's circumnavigation of the world as translated by Paula Spurlin Paige.

48 – John Rabe headed the Nazi party & International Committee during the Rape of Nanking. Considered the Oskar Schindler of the Pacific Theatre, he helped save thousands of Chinese citizens from marauding Japanese soldiers. Upon his return to Germany, he fell out of favor with the party for attempting to expose Japanese atrocities.

50 – April, 27 2007, Adrian Parsons circumcised himself in the performance piece "Shrapnel" at the *Supple* exhibition hosted by Washington, DC's Warehouse Galleries.

58 – Informed by a photograph in Iris Chang's *Rape of Nanking* and John Dower's *Embracing Defeat*.

67 – Several passages are taken from DeMorga's 1609 history of the Philippines.

72 – From the Anselm Kiefer exhibition at the Hirshorn, 2006.